SERMON OUTLINES
on

Prayer

Charles R. Wood

kregel
PUBLICATIONS

Grand Rapids, MI 49501

Sermon Outlines on Prayer by Charles R. Wood.

Copyright © 1994 by Charles R. Wood.

Published in 1994 by Kregel Publications, a division of Kregel, Inc., P.O. Box 2607, Grand Rapids, MI 49501. Kregel Publications provides trusted, biblical publications for Christian growth and service. Your comments and suggestions are valued.

Library of Congress Cataloging-in-Publication Data
Wood, Charles R. (Charles Robert), 1933–
   Sermon outlines on prayer / Charles R. Wood.
     p.   cm. (Easy-to-use sermon outline series)
   Includes index.
   1. Prayer—Sermons—Outlines, syllabi, etc. 2. Sermons, American—Outlines, syllabi, etc. 3. Baptists—Sermons—Outlines, syllabi, etc. I. Title. II. Series: Wood, Charles R. (Charles Robert), 1933– Easy-to-use sermon outline series.
BV210.2.W67   1994   251'.02—dc20   93-49094
                                    CIP

ISBN 0-8254-4140-4

3 4 5 6 7 / 07 06 05 04 03

Printed in the United States of America

Contents

List of Scripture Texts 5

Introduction 6

Take Your Burden to the Lord—Nehemiah 1:5–11 7

Just Keep Praying—Nehemiah 2:1–10 9

How Can I Say Thanks?—Psalm 147:1 11

Abominable Prayers—Proverbs 28:9 13

Prayer or Proclamation?—Matthew 6:5–8 15

Prayer: Problem or Power—Matthew 6:5–8 17

The Introduction to the Lord's Prayer—Matthew 6:9:15 19

The Invocation 21

The First Petition 22

The Second Petition 24

The Third Petition 25

The Fourth Petition 26

The Fifth Petition 27

The Sixth Petition 28

The Benediction 29

Pray Without Ceasing—1 Thessalonians 5:17 30

New Directions in Prayer—Matthew 6:9 31

Proper Priorities in Prayer—Matthew 6:9–10 33

Our Daily Bread—Matthew 6:11 35

Forgive Me; Forgive Me Not—Matthew 6:12, 14–15 37

A Look at Satan's "Playbook"—Matthew 6:13 39

Doxology—Matthew 6:13*b* 41

A Man Under Authority—Matthew 8:5–13; Luke 7:1–10 43

Our Lord's Prayer Life—Matthew 14:23 45

Of Puppy Dogs and Prayer—Matthew 15:21–28 47

Prayer and Faith—Matthew 21:22; Mark 11:24 49

How to Stay Out of Trouble—Matthew 26:41 51

The Pattern of Prayer—Luke 11:1–13 53

The Crowbar of Prayer—Luke 11:5–13 55

Don't Faint—Luke 18:1–8 57

3

The Man Who Prayed to Himself—Luke 18:9–14 59
Grab Your Bible and Let Us Pray—John 17:17 61
Prayer and the Will of God—Romans 8:26–27;
    Psalm 37:4; 1 John 3:22 63

List of Scripture Texts

Nehemiah 1:5–11 7

Nehemiah 2:1–10 9

Psalm 37:4 63

Psalm 147:1 11

Proverbs 28:9 13

Matthew 6:5–8 15

Matthew 6:5–8 17

Matthew 6:9–15 19

Matthew 6:9 31

Matthew 6:9–10 33

Matthew 6:11 35

Matthew 6:12, 14–15 37

Matthew 6:13 39

Matthew 6:13*b* 41

Matthew 8:5–13 43

Matthew 14:23 45

Matthew 15:21–28 47

Matthew 21:22 49

Matthew 26:41 51

Mark 11:24 49

Luke 7:1–10 43

Luke 11:1–13 53

Luke 11:5–13 55

Luke 18:1–8 57

Luke 18:9–14 59

John 17:17 61

Romans 8:26–27 63

1 Thessalonians 5:17 30

1 John 3:22 63

Introduction

As average, modern Christians, we have little affinity for prayer. Our experience is limited to a series of encounters in the midst of trials, and our knowledge of the potential hidden in meaningful communion with God is at best meager. The busy, time-starved times in which we live militate against a deepening practice of the presence of God.

As average, modern Christians, we are also hampered in attempting to develop a satisfactory prayer life by erroneous teaching that has too often been promulgated by well-intentioned preaching. A misunderstanding of one or two basic concepts has led to the belief that prayer is either a matter of prying things out of the grasp of a reluctant God or something specially reserved for the saintly "super Christian."

The outlines in this book reflect the underlying convictions that God is more willing to give than we are to receive and that any Christian can see significant accomplishment in prayer. Hopefully, messages preached with these outlines as their backbones will reflect those two truths.

The sermons here outlined are largely drawn from the New Testament. Although I do not question the relevance of Old Testament teaching on prayer, I find the New Testament teaching far fuller and deeper, influenced by concepts such as the indwelling presence of the Holy Spirit and the intercessory work of the Lord Jesus Christ. Further, there are a number of messages on the Lord's Prayer, that I believe to be a sample prayer.

The outlines in this volume are the product of my pulpit ministry, although my thinking and proclamation have been profoundly affected by a myriad of influences both past and present.

These are sermons designed to be preached, and they may be preached essentially "as is" without extensive further study. Time spent with the text and consultation of additional helps, however, can translate these messages into the personal expressions of the one preaching them. It is highly likely that careful study and preparation will enable the preacher to find several sermons in a single outline.

May our gracious Father be pleased to use these outlines to challenge many of His servants—and through them His people—to develop a disciplined, growing, and achieving prayer life.

CHARLES R. WOOD

Take Your Burden to the Lord
Nehemiah 1:5–11

Introduction:

Do you have a heavy burden bothering you? Would you really like to see something happen regarding it? Nehemiah can help you! He received word of the state of affairs in Jerusalem, he was deeply moved by those conditions, and he went to the Lord with his burden. His prayer is a pattern for handling our burdens.

I.   **Focus on God** (v. 5)
    A. Nehemiah gives us five facets on which to focus.
        1. "Lord"—Jehovah; self-existent, immutable God.
        2. "God of heaven"—dwells, reigns there; thus on earth.
        3. "Great God"—infinite in all perfections, filling all with His presence, exalted above all (majesty).
        4. "Terrible God"—dreaded by foes; revered by friends.
        5. "God that keepeth"—faithful to His obligation.
    B. We need a fresh view of God.

II. **Concentrate on Confession** (vv. 6–7)
    A. Nehemiah details aggravation of Israel's sins (v. 7).
        1. It was by a favored people.
        2. They sinned against God.
        3. They sinned against specific commandments of God.
        4. They sinned against dramatic circumstances showing God's power, etc.
    B. Nehemiah identifies himself in that sin (v. 6).
        1. It is not likely that he was guilty of much.
        2. A clear view of God makes us aware of sin.
        3. A readiness to face sin is a mark of spiritual state.

III. **Claim Your Grounds** (vv. 8–11)
    A. Notice the things he claimed:
        1. The name(s) of God.
        2. The promises of God—(v. 9).
        3. Their relationship to God—(v. 10a).
        4. The past history of God's working—(v. 10b).
    B. Notice the sincerity of the request:
        1. Others were united with him.
        2. The entreaty was urgent (language of entreaty is often redundant).

C. God is not dishonored by reminders of our grounds for prayer.
  1. It shows that we have learned something.
  2. It states that we depend on His character.

IV. **Make Your Request** (v. 11)
  A. Nehemiah knew what he wanted.
    1. He had already formulated plan.
    2. He wanted God's blessing on it.
    3. He had simple means of confirming.
  B. You need to be specific in your requests.
    1. Ask for what you want but do it conditioned by His will.
    2. When you don't know what you want, pray for clarity.

Conclusion:
Nehemiah has a message for you whose hearts are heavily burdened. Take your burden to the Lord in prayer and see these burdens lifted! Commit to practice the pattern of Nehemiah's prayer until the prayer is answered and the burden is lifted.

Just Keep Praying

Nehemiah 2:1–10

Introduction:

There is an old song, country and corny, that says, "Just keep on praying 'till the light breaks through." It was not very good music, but it is a very good suggestion. These are encouraging words as we seek to have our burdens lifted.

I. **Changing hearts is the work of God.**
    A. Nehemiah ran a great risk.
        1. Slaves were not to be sad in the presence of kings.
        2. He allowed emotions to show—could have cost his life.
    B. Artaxerxes granted him his request.
        1. He gave him everything he wanted and more.
        2. He appears very willing to do so.
    C. Only God can change hearts, but God *can* change hearts.
        1. See Proverbs 21:1.
        2. "You can't change people, but you can keep telling God on them."

II. **Prayer and waiting go together.**
    A. Nehemiah had to wait—Chisleu (Dec.) thru Nisan (April).
        1. This is one of shorter waits in Scripture.
        2. Remember Abraham, Hannah, David, etc.
    B. Remember: God does not work according to our timetable.
        1. He does not view time as we do.
        2. He works with the "fulness of time"—just the right moment.
    C. "You have not learned to pray until you have learned to wait."
        1. See Hebrews 10:36.
        2. God always has a purpose in His delays.

III. **Faith is not a substitute for planning or action.**
    A. Nehemiah had a plan in mind.
        1. He knew time length he needed (v. 6).
        2. He knew materials needed (v. 8).
        3. He had his request list all ready when prayer answered.

B. There is no problem with plans and action.
   1. They must be kept subordinate to the will of God (Nehemiah in ideal spot here—he had plan but couldn't act without king's approval).
   2. Prov. 3:5–6—don't sit immobilized—do what you can or know to do.
C. "Our prayers must be seconded by our serious efforts or else we mock God by them."

IV. Everything granted comes from the hand of God.
A. Nehemiah saw every grant as from God (v. 8).
   1. He knew everything depended on God.
   2. This becomes the secret of his success.
B. Without God's working in situation, disaster would have resulted.
   1. He could well have been killed for his trouble.
   2. He would at least have ended up frustrated.
C. "Thanksgivings are not so plentiful as prayers."

V. Expect opposition when you commit to God's will.
A. Sanballat and Tobiah are mentioned—opposition emerges (v. 10).
   1. Opposition reappears repeatedly in book (13 times).
   2. Prayer always involves opposition.
B. Note mention of them at Nehemiah's moment of triumph.
   1. This is not accidental placement.
   2. This is a frequent experience—opposition at time of triumph.
C. "When you walk by faith, you can expect to collide with those who walk by sight."

Conclusion:
Once you've committed to seeing a burden lifted, the realities begin to soak in. The experience of Nehemiah answers our objections and questions. "Just keep on praying 'till the light breaks through."

How Can I Say Thanks?

Psalm 147:1

Introduction:

The subject of gratitude is an enormous one. It needs exploration because we know so little about it and practice so little of it.

I. **Why should I be thankful?**
   A. Because of all I have to be thankful for.
   B. Because God commands me to be thankful.
      1. It honors Him.
      2. It reminds me of my dependence.
      3. It makes me focus on my blessings.
      4. It strengthens my testimony.
      5. It makes me a stronger Christian.

II. **For what should I be thankful?**
   A. Material blessings.
   B. Temporal blessings.
   C. Spiritual blessings.
   D. Things that don't happen.
   E. Problems, trials, and burdens, etc.
      1. They are a sign God is working in my life.
      2. They put me where miracles can take place.
      3. They develop spiritual graces in my life.

III. **What keeps me from being thankful?**
   A. Self-centeredness.
      1. "I have it coming to me anyhow."
      2. "I worked it out on my own."
      3. "I have it rougher than anyone" (self-pity).
   B. Unawareness.
      1. I am unmindful of blessings.
      2. I am indifferent.
      3. I am careless.
   C. Negative mind set.
      1. I am filled with bitterness.
      2. I am only able to see problems.
   D. Sin in the heart.
      1. Guilt denies God.
      2. My upset blocks gratitude.

IV. **To whom should I be grateful?**
   A. God—He is the ultimate source.
   B. I owe so much to others.

V. How can I say thanks?

A. By expressing it:
   1. In prayer.
   2. In testimony.
   3. To others.
B. By living in the light of what I have:
   1. Enjoying what I have rather than bemoaning what I don't.
   2. Refusing to entertain an ungrateful spirit.
   3. Continual counting of blessings.
C. By living for others:
   1. Much tangible gratitude can be shown to others.
   2. What God does for us we should pass on to others.
   3. What I have is of worth only as I share it.
D. By obeying what He has commanded:
   1. Real gratitude shows itself in doing what He wants.
   2. To be grateful and disobedient is hypocrisy.

Conclusion:

We have so much to be thankful for. God wants us to be thankful. Are you? Why not?

Abominable Prayers

Proverbs 28:9

Introduction:

Many people are concerned about hypocrisy. There are probably few areas where it shows more than in prayer. We must concern ourselves not with how we pray but with how we obey.

I. **Deafness**
   A. To "turn away from hearing the law" is more than a matter of not listening ("turneth away"—to "turn off").
   B. "Hearing"—to hear intelligently (with implication of attention, obedience), to discern, give ear to.
   C. "Law"—general word for the whole revelation of God's mind concerning faith and practice.
   D. To refuse to hear and heed the teaching of God regarding faith and practice is spiritual deafness.

II. **Determination**—There is always a measure of determination in refusing to obey.
   A. How do we turn our ears away?
      1. By ignoring it—this is inexcusable.
      2. By disobeying it—there is a deliberateness here that is frightening.
      3. By misinterpreting it—this is a possibility.
      4. Everyone has the right to interpretation, but none has the right to make a personal opinion an interpretation.
   B. Why do we turn our ears away? Because of:
      1. Disagreement.
      2. Weakness.
      3. Self-will.
      4. Inconvenience.

III. **Disregard**—When there is this determined deafness, God then disregards our prayers.
   A. Prayer becomes an "abomination."
      1. Strong word often used in Scripture—something disgusting, abhorrent.
      2. God has no regard to the prayer of the one who is ignoring His law.
   B. Is this just a "one-shot" teaching?
      1. We can base doctrine on single passage, but usually best not to do so.

    2. This has ample corroboration in:
       a. Proverbs 21:13
       b. Zechariah 7:11-13
       c. Psalm 66:18
       d. 1 Peter 3:7

C. Implications:
    1. "When we live in willful disobedience to any of God's commandments, we declare all our profession to be insincere . . . ."
    2. Why should one seek the favors of a sovereign whom he will not obey?
    3. God does not triffle with us; should we triffle with God?
    4. God cares nothing for reverence in the temple if He sees wickedness in the marketplace.

Conclusion:

To pray while disobeying is pure hypocrisy. We want to do things our own way, but we want God to do them our way also.

Prayer or Proclamation?

Matthew 6:5–8

Introduction:

Public prayer is problematic. It is so easy to lead a group in prayer and so hard to pray from the heart. Christ has some teaching for us on this subject.

I. **Condemnation**
   A. Jesus condemns their method.
      1. They stood in the synagogue (looking for prominence).
      2. They stood on the street-corners (plain view).
      3. Jesus does not condemn standing in general as it was a common practice.
   B. Jesus condemns their manner.
      1. Impression—"that they may be seen by men"—they were concerned with an impression.
      2. Impersonation—they were trying to give the impression that they were spiritual and pious.
      3. Intention—they were trying to make it look like they were so earnest that they couldn't wait.
   C. Jesus condemns their motive.
      1. Design—their end in view was to have the applause of men.
      2. Designation—Christ calls them hypocrites.
      3. Denunciation—He says that they have their reward already, thus ruling out future reward.

II. **Caution**
   A. We should be aware of similarity.
      1. We like to condemn the hypocrites and Pharisees.
      2. It is possible for us to be exactly like them.
      3. We must examine our own hearts in the light of the word.
   B. We should be aware of selfishness.
      1. This is a subtle problem in prayer.
      2. It is contrary to the communion with God.
   C. We should be aware of style.
      1. Form is an undue stress on what we say and how we say it before others.
      2. Time can become too important to us.

III. **Corrective**
   A. Jesus commends secrecy (v. 6).
      1. Meaning—to shut out other things (including the idea of recognition by others).
      2. The closet and the shut door are attitudes of heart and mind.
   B. Jesus commends sincerity (vv. 7, 8a).
      1. Prohibition—don't be like the heathen.
      2. Identify the vain repetitions (Hail Mary's, prayer wheels).
      3. Don't be like them:
         a. Either by doing what they do.
         b. Or by thinking you will be heard for much talk.
   C. Jesus commends simplicity (v. 8b).
      1. Remember the basic precondition—God knows all about your need before you ever get there.
      2. The accoutrements are not necessary at all.
      3. Prayer is a matter of fellowship between the individual and God.

Conclusion:
Nothing tests the reality of spiritual life more than being face to face with God in prayer.

Prayer: Problem or Power

Matthew 6:5–8

Introduction:

It would seem that prayer would be the Christian's great source of power. It can be a great source of power, but it can be a place of real problems. We must be careful in prayer because our sin nature can follow us right into the throne room. Nothing is safe from our sinfulness.

I. **The Problem of Prayer**
   A. Prayer can express selfishness.
      1. We tend to focus on the one who is praying.
         a. That which draws attention to self.
         b. That which advertises that we are praying.
      2. We tend to focus on personal wants/needs.
         a. It's amazing how selfish most of our praying actually is.
         b. The Christian's focus on others should show in prayer.
      3. We tend to define spirituality outwardly.
         a. By length/amount of prayer—saints of old prayed much because they were godly, not *vice versa*.
         b. Spirituality is always inward.
   B. Prayer can focus on form.
      1. We are too concerned with actual wording of prayer.
      2. We tend to stress time.
         a. We concentrate on length of time spent.
         b. We concentrate on regularity of time spent.

II. **The Power of Prayer**
   A. It is simply the individual approaching God.
      1. There is nothing mystical about prayer.
      2. It is communication between two persons.
   B. Powerful prayer involves:
      1. Exclusion
         a. Other people—mentally, not physically.
         b. Yourself.
         c. Real issue is sincerity more than secrecy.
      2. Realization
         a. Who and what God really is.
         b. The Fatherhood of God and all the relationships which that suggests.
         c. The ability of God to accomplish anything.

3. Confidence
   a. The confidence of a child with it's father.
   b. The realization that God wants to bless more than I want to be blessed ("prayer involves a basket, not a battering ram").
   c. The realization that He already knows what I need.

Conclusion:

Prayer can be a problem, but the real problem lies with our sinful nature. Prayer can be a source of power when we pray with reverence and confidence.

The Introduction to the Lord's Prayer

Matthew 6:9–15

Introduction:
What we call the "Lord's prayer" is really the disciples' prayer, given by the Lord in response to their request that He teach them to pray.

I. **Its Relevance**
    A. They had prayer problems—desired to know His secret of success in prayer.
       1. Even the disciples had some problems.
       2. Everyone has problems in prayer, particularly the inability to find time for and to concentrate in prayer.
    B. Is it for today?
       1. Misunderstanding makes it a future teaching for a postponed kingdom.
       2. A proper understand makes it relevant to today.

II. **Its Structure**
    A. Outline:
       1. Introduction to the prayer.
       2. Petitions.
          a. Hallowed be thy name.
          b. Thy kingdom come.
          c. Thy will be done on earth as in heaven.
          d. Give us this day our daily bread.
          e. Forgive us our debts (as we forgive our debtors).
          f. Deliver us from evil.
       3. Conclusion of the prayer.
    B. Sequence:
       1. Begins with worship.
       2. Moves into supplication.
       3. Closes with a note of praise.
    C. Noteworthy items:
       1. Different from most of our praying.
       2. Strongly God-centered in outlook (note emphasis on God in 4 of 9 parts).

III. **Its Importance**
    A. It was given as a sample.
       1. Note the disciples' request (Luke 11:1).
       2. This is "how to pray," not a prayer.

B. It provides a pattern for our praying.
   1. Note its simplicity.
   2. Note its perfection as an expression of spiritual feelings—there is a place here for every Christian emotion.
   3. It is really an outline form for prayer.

Conclusion:

The Lord's prayer contains all the elements essential for prayer. It provides us with an ideal model for our prayer.

The Invocation

Introduction:

In the opening words of the Lord's prayer proper, there are two particularly important things pointed out.

I. **An Expression of Relationship—"Our Father."**
   A. It implies sonship.
      1. Bible teaches fatherhood of God through creation.
      2. Bible teaches fatherhood of God through adoption.
   B. It implies dependency.
      1. The very act of prayer indicates a deep sense of dependency.
      2. Only persons who truly realize their dependence upon the Father can pray.
   C. It implies communion.
      1. Notice the number of the pronouns—first person plural rather than singular.
      2. There is a striking contrast with much of our praying—we are concerned for ourselves alone.

II. **An Expression of Revelation—"Which art in heaven."**
   A. There is a proper translation.
      1. It really reads "who art in the heavens."
      2. The reason is that there are three heavens in the Word:
         a. Jeremiah 4:25—atmosphere around earth.
         b. Matthew 24:29—celestial sphere.
         c. 2 Corinthians 12:2—place of God's abode.
   B. This translation has meaning.
      1. "The God of the far distant heaven" speaks of transcendence.
      2. "The God of the near heavens" speaks of immanence (nearness).
      3. Both are absolutely necessary.

Conclusion:

The Christian is reminded by the opening of the Lord's prayer of two great facts: we are related to a God who has revealed Himself.

The First Petition

Introduction:

The Lord's prayer is a sample of prayer for today. It has a three-part structure which begins with worship. "Our Father who art in heaven" is the dependent prayer of children prayed in communion with a great and reachable God.

I. **The Meaning of the Petition**
   A. "Hallowed"
      1. We should reverence it.
      2. We should hold it in esteem.
   B. "Thy name"
      1. The name of God was used for revelation of God in Old Testament.
         a. Jehovah-jireh—Lord will provide.
         b. Jehovah-rapha—Lord that healeth.
         c. Jehovah-nissi—Lord our banner.
         d. Jehovah-shalom—Lord our peace.
         e. Jehovah-ra-ah—Lord our shepherd.
         f. Jehovah-tsidekenu—Lord our righteousness.
      2. Being used to reveal His character, "Name" comes to stand for God Himself.
   C. Summary—The first concern in prayer: "May who and what you are come to be reverenced by people everywhere."

II. **The Importance of the Petition**
   A. It was Christ's chief aim.
      1. John 17:4.
      2. His whole life on earth was dedicated to depicting God in such a way as to glorify Him.
   B. It is the aim of Scripture.
      1. Bible tells us what we need to know about many things.
      2. Supreme in it is the glory of God.
   C. It is the chief end of man.
      1. Why are we here? To glorify God.
      2. It is more important than anything else because it includes everything else.

III. **The Method of the Petition**
   A. His name must be made known.
      1. You can't reverence what you don't know.
      2. This gives a missionary emphasis to the prayer.

B. We should give it proper representation.
   1. We are the only contact that many people have with Gospel or with God.
   2. Our responsibility is great to glorify God.

Conclusion:

When we pray, "Hallowed be thy name," we pray for an important thing. But it is a prayer of personal responsibility. Let us be sure we reverence God's Name before we pray that others reverence Him.

The Second Petition

Introduction:

Praying "thy kingdom come" should involve more than the mere mouthing of words. A most important concept is in view.

I. **What is the kingdom of God?**
   A. Secular sphere.
      1. A king rules and reigns.
      2. His sphere of influence is in His kingdom.
   B. Spiritual realm.
      1. It is the rule and reign of God.
      2. It is the sphere over which it is extended.

II. **What is the kingdom like?**
   A. The kingdom is realized (cf. Luke 17:21).
      1. Wherever Christ rules and reigns in the heart, the kingdom is come.
      2. In this sense the kingdom has come and is realized.
   B. The kingdom is coming—we are told to pray "thy kingdom come."
      1. It is the visible manifestation of the realized kingdom.
      2. Positions in regard to the kingdom:
         a. Postmillenialism—world gets better and better until Lord finally comes with kingdom already established.
         b. Amillenialism—there is no millennium.
         c. Premillenialism—there is coming a period of 1,000 years when Christ will rule and reign upon earth.

III. **How is the kingdom brought?**
   A. The invisible kingdom comes through submission.
      1. The warfare of two kingdoms involves us.
      2. We must own Christ as Lord as well as Savior.
   B. The visible kingdom comes at God's appointment.
      1. We are not privileged to know the day nor hour.
      2. We can win the lost and pray to hasten it.

Conclusion:

Let us pray and work for His kingdom to come (both in hearts and in the world).

The Third Petition

Introduction:

In the Lord's prayer we are praying to our heavenly Father which indicates we are related to Him. In the first three petitions we are concerned with Him and with His glory.

I. **God has a will.**
   A. Definition: New Testament words for "will."
      1. There is a general will—the plan and purpose of God for the world and for people.
      2. But the specific word is used here—what God wishes to happen.
   B. Knowledge of the will.
      1. The general contents of God's will can be known.
      2. It is not always possible to understand it.

II. **God's will is perfectly done in heaven.**
   A. Heaven is given to us as the pattern for the doing of God's will.
      1. Angels are the subjects there.
      2. This is the ultimate in performance of His will.
   B. Four ways in which His will is done.
      1. Universally—everyone there does it.
      2. Immediately—it is done as soon as commanded.
      3. Without exception—not only does everyone do what they are supposed to do, but they do *all* that they are supposed to.
      4. Willingly—their service is joyful and in a willing spirit.

III. **It should be performed in the earth.**
   A. Current situation.
      1. Overall plan of God is being worked out.
      2. What God wishes to happen is not being done.
      3. Truly the petition is needed today.
   B. Ultimate accomplishment.
      1. A time coming when it will be done on earth as in heaven.
      2. Christ shall have His perfect way then.
   C. Present possibility.
      1. It can be in the realm of men's hearts.
      2. It can be done there as in heaven.
      3. This involves total personal surrender.
      4. We should not, dare not pray this way unless we are willing for His will.

Conclusion:

Are you willing for God's will to be done? Unless you are, it is best not to pray this petition.

The Fourth Petition

Introduction:

Bread was the "staff of life" for people in Bible times. This petition deals with the supply of our daily bread.

I. **It demonstrates dependence upon God.**
   A. This is shown in the introduction of prayer and made specific here.
   B. Such dependence builds Christian character.
      1. It is contrary to world's viewpoint.
      2. We grow strong by dependence.

II. **It demonstrates confidence in Him.**
   A. It assumes He is able to provide.
      1. We go where we are likely to get help.
      2. Thus we recognize His rulership in natural world.
   B. It shows our willingness to accept His provision.
      1. The meaning of term for bread—"Staff of life."
      2. It covers whole area of material provisions.
      3. It leaves determination up to Him (quantity, type of provision, etc.).
      4. When we pray thus, we show that we will take what He gives us.

III. **It demonstrates God's method of operation.**
   A. The interpretation is difficult, but it at least means— "Give us today what we need for today."
   B. God's method.
      1. He gives us what we need.
      2. He gives us what we need as we need it.
      3. He wants us to come to Him for it.
   C. It is typified by manna in Old Testament.
      1. God gave all they needed, not wanted, one day at a time.
      2. God *never* promises to give all we want.

Conclusion:

We should ask for what we need. We should leave it up to the Lord and not worry about tomorrow.

The Fifth Petition

Introduction:
Forgiveness is the core of our Christianity. Unfortunately, it is not always common to our Christian lives.

I. **What We Are Dealing With Here**
   A. There are two uses of "sin" in Scripture.
      1. One is the principle of sin.
      2. The other is the practice of sin—individual acts.
   B. The latter is used here.
      1. "Transgressions" indicates acts.
      2. As a family prayer, it only leaves room for specific acts.

II. **Implied Confession**
   A. There is a need.
      1. To pray "forgive" involves admission of guilt.
      2. God desires us to thus pray—He knows but He wants us to confess and own up to it.
   B. There is an urgency.
      1. Restoration of fellowship depends on it.
      2. It is oftened much ignored today.

III. **Shows Continuity**
   A. Verse 11 says—"Give us day by day our needed bread."
      1. It indicates daily recognition of need.
      2. It indicates constant dependence.
   B. The "and" relates this phrase to the previous.
      1. It seems to attach this to the idea of repetition.
      2. Forgiveness and confession need to be constant.

IV. **The Single Standard**
   A. There is a great misunderstanding here.
      1. We can't be forgiven on basis of our forgiveness.
      2. This is a family prayer, and we are not seeking forgiveness of sin as a principle.
   B. This is a searchlight.
      1. God's viewpoint is illustrated in Matthew 18:21.
      2. God will not have a double standard.
         a. We cannot ask one thing of Him and give others another.
         b. Must treat others way we want them to treat us.

V. **How to Be Unforgiven**
   A. Failure to forgive others will hinder our own forgiveness.

B. It does not invalidate 1 John 1:9.
   1. This is always true.
   2. It implies that it must be done in right way.
C. There is a logical relationship.
   1. "If I regard iniquity in my heart, the Lord will not hear me"—Psalm 68:18.
   2. An unforgiving spirit is iniquity.
   3. God will not hear my prayer for forgiveness if I harbor the sin of unforgiveness in my heart.

Conclusion:
Are you willing for God's forgiveness to be extended to you on the same basis as you forgive others? If not, why not?

The Sixth Petition

Introduction:
Christianity is designed to affect the whole of life. The Lord's prayer covers every aspect of living.

I. **Is there a contradiction here?**
    A. It appears to contradict James 1:13.
    B. There are two meanings of "temptation."
       1. One means circumstances of trial—James 1:2.
       2. One means solicitation to evil—James 1:14–15.

II. **There are two petitions.**
    A. "Lead us not into temptation"—keep us from circumstances.
       1. These can be good or ill—James 1:9–11.
       2. This demands sincere cooperation on our part.
       3. Is this always answered?—no.
          a. Virtue needs choice to develop.
          b. Strength comes through standing—James 1:3–4.
    B. "Deliver us from evil"—keep us from falling to evil solicitation.
       1. This covers when evil enters into circumstances.
       2. This shows our desire for deliverance.
          a. This too needs cooperation.
          b. The method is dealt with in Ephesians 6:10–18.
       3. This can become a reality in life.

Conclusion:
If you will pray for deliverance from evil, then you should keep your distance from it.

The Benediction

Introduction:

There is some debate about whether or not these phrases ought to be in the text. They are certainly in accord with the general tenor of Scripture.

I. **Thine is the kingdom.**
   A. This is kingdom truth.
      1. There is a visible kingdom.
      2. There is an invisible kingdom.
   B. "Thy kingdom come."
      1. The visible is not yet realized.
      2. The invisible is not spread to widest possible area.
   C. "Thine is the kingdom."
      1. It is now present in hearts.
      2. World will ultimately be under His sway.

II. **Thine is the power.**
   A. There is proof of the statement.
      1. All power belongs to Christ—Matthew 28:18.
      2. What is its source?—Psalm 147:1–5.
   B. Reason for asking "because thine is the power."
   C. It is an implication of faith.
      1. It is a necessity—Matthew 21:22.
      2. This is a declaration.

III. **Thine is the glory.**
   A. It is ultimately true.
      1. Psalm 29:2.
      2. Psalm 57:5.
   B. It must be objectively applied.
      1. We must practice confession.
      2. We must practice real belief.
   C. It has practical import.
      1. It involves searching.
      2. It is one reason why so much prayer not answered.

Conclusion:

God will ultimately rule in power and glory. Is He ruling in your heart? Do you own His power? Do you give Him the glory?

Pray Without Ceasing
1 Thessalonians 5:17

Introduction:

We must oppose any teaching that puts good Christianity out of the reach of the average Christian. Anyone can be a good Christian.

I. **The context**
   A. Rejoice evermore.
   B. It will take a lot of praying.
   C. Joy and prayer produces thanks.

II. **The content**
   A. Promise
      1. There is never an unacceptable time.
      2. We can never pray too often.
      3. We can never pray too much.
   B. Precept
      1. Never abandon prayer.
      2. Never stop praying for a particular thing.
      3. Develop a spirit of prayer.
   C. Caution
      1. Never be where you can't pray.
      2. Let your actions be a continuation of prayer.

III. **The challenge**
   A. The Lord always deserves worship.
   B. We always need a blessing.
   C. We are always in danger of temptation.
   D. We always have needs/wants.
   E. There are always those who need your prayers.

Conclusion:

The church needs more prayer. Your Christian friends need more prayer. The world in which we live needs more prayer. Will you take the challenge?

New Directions in Prayer
Matthew 6:9

Introduction:
"Because we know not what to pray for as we ought, He here helps our infirmities, by putting words into our mouths." There is much confusion on prayer. It has become empty, vain, repetitious, and it has been loaded up with difficulties never intended.

I. **"Our Father"**
   A. It shows adoption.
      1. A common Biblical concept—we are His children.
      2. It is stated Ephesians 1:5 and Galatians 4:6.
      3. It introduces a designed analogy.
      4. Remember, He is not an angry deity but a loving father.
   B. It shows advocacy.
      1. It is one who represents to aid another.
      2. It is taught in 1 John 2:1.
      3. It was part of His post-resurrection ministry.
      4. He seeks and desires the answer of our prayers.
   C. It shows access.
      1. We are given an open door through Him.
      2. It is taught in Ephesians 2:18 and 3:12.
      3. It is one of the blessings of "childhood."
      4. He is more ready to hear us than we ever are to approach Him.
   D. It shows His attitude toward us because He is a father.
      1. He will pity us.
      2. He will spare us whenever possible.
      3. He will make the best of us.
      4. He will deny us nothing commensurate with His will and our best interests.

II. **"Which art in Heaven"**
   A. It shows purity.
      1. "In heaven"—spirit realm—prayer must be spiritual in order to please Him.
      2. We must come with purity—sin confessed.
      3. We must come with pure motives (submitted to what has just been said).
   B. It shows perspective.
      1. He sees all.

2. It grants a perspective we don't have.
3. It accounts for what may appear to be unanswered prayer.
C. It shows power.
   1. We pray to One with infinite power.
   2. He is willing and able.
   3. He is able and willing.
D. It shows His pleasure (the way in which He would have us approach Himself).
   1. Comprehensively—He is our Father. There is nothing outside the scope of His concern.
   2. Freely—we need never hesitate or come through anyone else.
   3. Boldly—we can enter directly in to Him ("burst in").
   4. Reverently—we deal with the King of the Ages so we come in the light of His majesty.

Conclusion:

We need a new direction in prayer that stresses God's willingness. God is more willing to hear than we are to speak. God is more willing to answer than we are to ask. Maybe we should get away from some of the confusing teaching and just say, "Our Father, which art in heaven."

Proper Priorities in Prayer

Matthew 6:9–10

Introduction:

There are six petitions in the Lord's Prayer, and the first three pertain to God's honor. This teaches us, ". . . seek ye first the kingdom of God . . . and all these things shall be added unto you."

I. **"Hallowed be thy Name"**
   A. The point of the petition.
      1. "Hallowed"—sanctified, set apart.
      2. "Name"—representative of the person.
      3. "May you be glorified."
   B. The priority of the petition.
      1. Most important that God be glorified.
      2. "In prayer our thoughts and affections should be carried out most to the glory of God."
   C. The petition.
      1. That God may be glorified.
         a. By my prayers.
         b. By my person.
         c. By my performance.
      2. The glory of God supreme.
   D. The petition practicalized.
      1. We are asking for what we know will be granted.
      2. Why ask for what is certain?
         a. It shows our submission to His purposes.
         b. It makes us part of the process.

II. **"Thy kingdom come"**
   A. The point of the petition.
      1. The rule and reign of God.
      2. The area where God rules and reigns.
   B. The parameters of the petition.
      1. Present—a spiritual kingdom in the hearts of people.
      2. Future—a physical kingdom on the earth.
      3. Ultimate—a literal kingdom over all.
   C. The purpose of the petition.
      1. May your kingdom come.
      2. May it be embraced by all, owned by all.
   D. The practicalities of the petition.
      1. We should view this prayer as a pattern of prayer.
      2. We can't pray Lord's prayer without this phrase.
      3. We can't pray it without willingness to be involved.

III. **"Thy will be done"**
   A. The presupposition in the petition.
      1. Underlies all other petitions.
      2. Starts off on right foot.
   B. The pattern in the petition.
      1. Not just "May Thy will be done."
      2. Adds idea of on earth as it already is in heaven.
   C. The particulars of the petition.
      1. Done immediately.
      2. Done completely.
      3. Done willingly.
   D. The petition personalized.
      1. Can't pray it until submitted to it.
      2. Can't be submitted to it without obedience.
      3. Can't be obedient to it without conformity to Word.

Conclusion:
The Lord's prayer, ". . . has much in a little, and it is requisite that we acquaint ourselves with the sense and meaning of it, for it is used acceptably no further than it is used with understanding and without vain repetition" How often do we pray with real understanding of prayer? How often do we begin with what is really important?

Our Daily Bread

Matthew 6:11

Introduction:

The Bible is an amazing book. It was written two to four thousand years ago, but it still speaks clearly to our day. Several subjects are "big ticket" right now in our society: self-direction, independence; sufficiency and what comprises it; and security and how it is attained. This petition clearly speaks to all three points.

I. **The Truth It Expresses**
   A. "Bread"
      1. This is the central theme.
      2. It has to do with our being and subsistence.
   B. "Our bread"
      1. It refers to that which belongs to us.
      2. It implies honesty and industry.
   C. "Our daily bread"
      1. It is based on economic system of the times.
      2. It is the bread that we need for the only time that we have.
   D. "Give . . . our daily bread"
      1. It directs our attention to our source.
      2. It declares our dependence on God.
   E. "Give us . . . our daily bread"
      1. It teaches corporateness in prayer.
      2. It implies development of compassion.
   F. "Give us this day our daily bread"
      1. Our requests must be renewed daily.
      2. It forces us to daily communion.

II. **The Issues It Addresses**
   A. Man's self-directedness and independence.
      1. Modern man wants independence.
      2. The petition forces us to recognize our source.
   B. Man's struggle with sufficiency (how much is enough?).
      1. Man can't find enough.
         a. "When all you've ever wanted isn't enough."
         b. It is behind much of the restlessness of our day.
      2. It speaks of sufficiency—"daily bread."
         a. "It is a bread convenient for us."
         b. "It is a bread agreeable to our condition."
      3. Sufficient is what He gives, and what He gives is sufficient (prayer is for our needs, not our greeds).

C. Man's struggle for security.
   1. Man seeks it dililgently—security is having the future assured.
   2. God gives is differently.
      a. He promises daily supply (today's for today and tomorrow's for tomorrow).
      b. He keeps us in constant dependence.
      c. The other side is that we see new mercies every day.
      d. "We have from God the supply of every day in that day according to what that day requires."
   3. Our security is in our source and the sufficience of His supply.

Conclusion:

It is not wrong to plan for the future, but it is wrong to be anxious about the future and wrong to find security in those plans. Remember: our Source is where we find sufficiency and security. Our sufficiency is what our Source supplies. Our security is in the sufficiency of our Source.

Forgive Me; Forgive Me Not

Matthew 6:12, 14–15

Introduction:

It is often held that most of us suffer from self-concept problems. The Bible certainly appears to disagree, as this passage shows.

I. **"And forgive us our debts . . . ."**
    A. What is in view here?
        1. Two words are used.
            a. "Trespasses"—idea of doing wrong.
            b. "Debt"—idea of something unpaid.
        2. Many commentators prefer stress of "debts."
            a. It puts emphasis on things undone.
            b. We are better at confessing what we have done than what we have left undone.
            c. What do we owe God?—obedience!
    B. Why is this necessary?
        1. From God's standpoint—to maintain our relationship with Him.
        2. From our standpoint—to retain a measure of peace.
    C. Note the connection in the passage—"and."
        1. It ties in to last verse.
        2. There is something in view for each day.

II. **"As we forgive our debtors."**
    A. Is this legal ground?
        1. Note prayer carefully.
            a. It says "Our Father."
            b. This is the prayer of the saved.
        2. This has nothing to do with earning salvation, but rather with the believer's daily walk.
    B. Note the clear statements of Scripture:
        1. Matthew 18:21ff
        2. Mark 11:25–26
        3. Luke 6:37; 17:3–5
        4. Ephesians 4:32
        5. Colossians 3:13
    C. This is evidential in nature.
        1. Our willingness to forgive others is clear indication that we have been forgiven ourselves.
        2. Our unwillingness to forgive others is indication that at least we don't understand forgiveness.

III. **"For if ye forgive men ... but if ye forgive not men ...."**—How failure to forgive others can block our own forgiveness.
   A. It shows the kind of hypocrisy the Lord hates and resists.
   B. It shows that we minimize our sin while magnifying the sins of others.
   C. It shows we don't understand key doctrinal issues such as grace and forgiveness.
   D. It ignores the "golden rule."
   E. It keeps us so preoccupied with wrongs that we are not open to His working in us.

Conclusion:

We should always be ready and willing to pray this prayer: "Lord, forgive my faults and failures in the same way I forgive the faults and failures of others. Lord, forgive my faults and failures to the same degree I forgive the faults and failures of others."

A Look at Satan's "Playbook"

Matthew 6:13

Introduction:
"Watch out for temptation; the more you see, the better it looks."

"Few speed records are broken by people running from temptation."

"One half the trouble of this life can be traced to saying yes too quickly, and not saying no soon enough."

I. **"Lead us not into temptation"**
    A. This is a plea for prevention.
    B. It involves at least three things:
        1. Don't let Satan loose around us.
        2. Don't leave us to ourselves.
        3. Don't leave us victims of circumstances.

II. **"But deliver us from evil"**
    A. It is a prayer for deliverance.
    B. We need deliverance from the evil one.
    C. We need deliverance from sin.
        1. The corruption that is in the world through lust.
        2. The evil of our own hearts.
        3. The will and work of evil people.

III. **A Look at Satan's "Playbook"** (Proverbs 7:6–23)—It deals with moral evil but gives us idea of how Satan operates in general in the realm of temptation.
    A. Temptation is strongest when the decision to do right is not made beforehand (6–7).
        1. We need clear moral standards to guide conduct.
        2. A lack of such standards is "moral immaturity."
        3. Many are committed to neither good nor evil.
    B. Temptation is strengthened when we underestimate evil and flirt with the temptation (8–9).
        1. We chose our own path to moral defeat.
        2. It is always dangerous to underestimate the power of evil.
    C. Our failure in temptation is always just a choice away (10–12).
        1. Evil lurks absolutely everywhere.
        2. Sin is always aggressive.

3. It is the main sources of enticement.
   a. In the world system of those around us.
   b. In the internal sinful desires of the flesh.
D. Temptation entices through flattery and fantasy (vv. 13–17).
   1. Temptation begins as a battle for the mind.
   2. Temptation always paints picture.
   3. Temptation always flatters.
E. Temptation always includes rationalization and deception (vv. 18–21).
   1. Rationalization: imputing a good purpose to something inherently wrong.
   2. We are geniuses at coming up with good reasons for bad actions.
   3. Evil always tries to convince us that:
      a. No one will ever know.
      b. There will be no consequences.
F. Temptation succeeds when we refuse to think about the rightness of our actions (v. 22).
   1. We choose our own failures.
   2. Choice is usually made suddenly and without thought.
G. Falling to temptation always has a price (vv. 22–23).
   1. It causes broken fellowship with God.
   2. It causes tarnished legacy for family.
   3. It causes loss of testimony before others.
   4. It causes loss of self-respect.

Conclusion:

This petition is backed by good reasons: the discomfort and trouble of enduring temptations, the danger of being overcome by them, the guilt and grief that follow succumbing to them, and the loss that comes as a result of falling to them. The person pursuing Godliness makes every effort to keep pure—not to get away with as much as possible.

Doxology

Matthew 6:13*b*

Introduction:

A doxology is an expression of praise to God. It is usually either in the form of a prayer itself or at the end of a prayer. There is a big argument about whether or not this phrase should be in the text. It does fit the context beautifully, so we can assume it belongs.

I. **It presses the prayer into perspective.**
- A. Note how it attaches to the petitions:
    1. "Thy kingdom come—for thine is the kingdom."
    2. "Thy will be done—for thine is the power."
    3. "Hallowed by Thy name—for thine is the glory."
- B. It makes the petitions meaningful.
    1. The kingdom is His.
        a. So we can pray for it to come.
        b. It will come in His own good time.
    2. The power is His.
        a. He can give us what we need for our bodies.
        b. He can forgive our debts.
        c. He can give victory over temptation.
        d. He can deliver us from evil.
    3. The glory is His.
        a. He alone is worthy of praise.
        b. He is our hope of glory.

II. **It terminates the prayer with praise.**
- A. The doxology turns the prayer into praise.
    1. Praise is contained in every petition; doxology makes praise the culminating point of the prayer.
    2. The doxology bases the prayer on His character.
        a. We don't ask to be heard for anything in ourselves.
        b. We ask to be heard for His character, Name, and promises.
    3. Praise expresses faith and bridges the gap between earth and heaven.
- B. Praise is a significant factor in prayer.
    1. "It is just . . . that we praise God. Not because He needs it, but because He deserves it."

2. "A true saint never thinks he can speak honorably enough of God."
3. "Thanksgiving from man to God is as essential an element of prayer as any giving of good things from God to man."

III. It forces the prayer into practice.
A. If God really is king, then we must fear and obey Him.
   1. We dare not ascribe kingdom to anyone else.
   2. We dare not yield to any competitor for the crown.
B. If the power really is God's, then we must live with faith in that truth.
   1. He has the power to preserve us from evil.
   2. He has the power to care for our eternal destinies.
   3. He has the power to provide for our temporal needs (why is it so easy to trust Him for eternity and so difficult to trust Him for temporal things?).
C. If the glory really is God's, then we must ascribe glory to Him.
   1. By our lips.
   2. By our lives.
   3. By our bodies.

Conclusion:
"The address and the doxology bind the petitions together into the perfect prayer. All flow out of the address—He is our Father, He will hear the prayer of His children. All rise in faith to the doxology—His is the kingdom, and the power, and the glory." "The best pleading with God lies in praising Him."

A Man Under Authority

Matthew 8:5–13; Luke 7:1–10

Introduction:

This story does not directly deal with prayer, but it touches on the most vital aspect of answered prayer—faith. He was a Gentile and a captain in the hated Roman army, but he teaches us a great deal about that faith which achieves.

I. **The Man**
   A. Note what we are told:
      1. He loved his servant ("my boy").
      2. He nursed his servant.
      3. He loved the Jewish nation.
      4. He built the Jews a synagogue.
      5. He became a proselyte of the Jewish faith.
   B. It paints us a picture of:
      1. A tender master.
      2. A considerable citizen.
      3. A lover of God.
   C. It teaches us a valuable lesson.
      1. All this is where least expected.
      2. Our calling and position in life are no excuse for sin—if we are in a place where we can't live for God, we ought not to be in that place; otherwise we are responsible to live for God in that place.
      3. We must stop excusing ourselves and come clean.

II. **His Manner**
   A. It was marked by great humility.
      1. It was shown by:
         a. Sending others (Luke).
         b. His statement.
         c. His not wanting Christ to come under his roof.
      2. It was derived from:
         a. A deep insight into his own heart.
         b. He saw what others did not or would not see.
   B. Teaches us a valuable lesson.
      1. The greater the humility, the greater the possibility.
         a. Of prayer—why pray if you are almighty.
         b. Of answer—why believe if you are self-confident.
      2. His humility enhances his faith.

III. His Mission
A. He came to Christ in behalf of his servant.
   1. He was suffering miserably.
   2. It is called palsy—probably MS or Parkinson's, etc.
B. Note that he came to Christ.
   1. He had a need he wanted met.
   2. He knew where he was likely to get help.

IV. His Method
A. He sends someone else to represent him.
B. He comes with total courtesy.
   1. He won't ask Christ to violate Jewish tradition.
   2. He asks nothing for himself.
C. He says, "I understand authority."
   1. "I also am under authority—my authority is derived but absolute.
   2. You have authority—Yours is also derived (from God) but absolute.

V. His Message
A. Some incidental truths here:
   1. Do good to your enemies.
   2. No one is beyond the reach of the Gospel.
   3. Christ is the place to go in the time of need.
   4. He shows obvious evidence of the kinds of change that should mark salvation.
   5. He recognized God's power and authority.
B. Basic truths in regard to prayer:
   1. He believed that Christ (God) can do anything in any way He chooses.
   2. He was willing for Christ (God) to do what he wanted in any way Christ might choose.

Conclusion:
Jesus said, ". . . I have not found so great faith, no, not in Israel." We claim we believe that God can do anything, but we balk at allowing Him to do things when and how He wishes. Do we really believe what we claim? Would this Centurion outrank you when it comes to faith?

Our Lord's Prayer Life

Matthew 14:23

Introduction:

In studying Christ's teaching on prayer, the lessons of His own example are very instructive. Let's look at His prayer life and draw some conclusions from it.

I. **The Passages Involved**
   A. Matthew 14:23
   B. Mark 1:35; 6:46
   C. Luke 4:42; 5:16; 11:1

II. **Observations on the Passages**
   A. He drew apart to pray.
      1. It is characteristic of all passages.
      2. He broke away from the crowd.
      3. He needed to get away even from His own.
   B. He went to some specific place.
      1. It was not always the same.
      2. Mountains figure prominently—why?
         a. It was good place to get away from crowd.
         b. It was geographically near God.
         c. He enjoyed mountains.
   C. We are sure He prayed often.
      1. We have enough glimpses to know this.
      2. It may account for disciples' lack of watchfulness in garden—the fact that He was in the habit.
   D. There was no specific time set for prayer.
      1. Matthew 14:23—evening
      2. Mark 1:35—morning
      3. Luke 4:42—day
      4. Luke 6:12—all night
      5. Luke 11:1—day
   E. His prayer was genuine.
      1. We must not conceive of it as symbolical or merely instructive.
      2. He prayed because He needed to pray.

III. **Lessons from His Prayer Life**
   A. If He needed to pray, how much more do we!
   B. We need to get apart regularly to pray.
      1. We need a place where the distracting press of life doesn't bother us.

2. We need to get away even from our own family.
3. He sought places where crowd wouldn't follow.
C. The life of prayer is essentially a lonely one.
1. No one can share it with us.
2. Prayer is lonely for humans, but fellowship with God.
D. He had to *make* a place for it in life; so will we.
1. It didn't just come naturally to Him.
2. There needs to be provision of the more formal time.
E. There is no set time for prayer, but we are advantaged by setting some time alone with the Lord.

Conclusion:

Christ's own prayer life teaches us much about prayer in general. We can't pray just like He did, but we need to learn from Him.

Of Puppy Dogs and Prayer
Matthew 15:21–28

Introduction:
We ask, "What did you do that for?" We do some things for no purpose. Christ never did! There was always purpose behind His acts, and sometimes more than one purpose. The story here is a case in point.

I.   **The Story**
   A. Christ seeking refuge.
      1. From popular enthusiasm.
      2. From Pharisaic opposition.
   B. On borders of Israel.
   C. Event may have covered more than one day.
   D. Woman was not a Jew (heathen, Canaanite).

II. **The Difficulties**
   A. Christ teaches the woman something.
      1. She has no right to come to Him.
      2. She calls Him by wrong name at first.
      3. She must learn proper relationship.
      4. Other Gentiles come with no problem, but likely something being taught here.
   B. Christ teaches the disciples something.
      1. Illustration of other teaching.
         a. Given in precept.
         b. Given in parable.
      2. Ideal living illustration of Luke 18:1.

III. **The Purpose: ". . . men ought always to pray and not to faint."**
   A. We should not faint instead of praying.
      1. She had dark, depressing circumstances.
      2. She was admittedly unworthy—Gentile, Canaanite, Greek.
      3. There are always more reasons not to pray than there are to pray.
   B. We should not faint about praying.
      1. The conduct of the disciples was a deterrent.

2. The silence of Christ was a deterrent.
   a. God's initial silence means neither.
      —deafness to our request
      —denial of what we seek
   b. Christ's "rough" answer had seeds of encouragement.
3. The narrow doctrine was a deterrent.
C. We should not faint while praying.
   1. She kept pursuing.
   2. She kept persisting (not presumptuous).
      a. "The mouth of faith can never be closed."
      b. Faith says, "I can get this, but even if I don't, I won't turn away."

Conclusion:

We urgently need to learn, ". . . men ought always to pray and not to faint." We faint instead of praying. We faint about praying and end up with half-hearted prayers. We faint while praying if we don't get what we want instantly. We must commit to prayer, to prayer no matter what, and to prayer until there is an answer or the burden is lifted.

Prayer and Faith

Matthew 21:22; Mark 11:24

Introduction:

Matthew 9:29 says, ". . . according to your faith be it unto you." Is it all as simple as that, or is there something more to this matter of faith, especially as it relates to prayer?

I. **The Demand of Faith**
    A. There is no point to prayer without faith (Heb. 11:6).
        1. Why pray if no belief that God exists?
        2. Why pray if no belief that He responds to us?
    B. We are specifically told that belief is required for answered prayer.
        1. This is something we assume.
        2. The more faith, the more likely to receive an answer.
    C. Answers to prayer may be in proportion to faith (Matt. 9:29).
        1. May mean, "You'll get what you believe you'll get."
        2. May mean, "You'll get as much as you believe you'll get."

II. **The Distortion of Faith**
    A. "You gotta believe."
        1. Faith is subjective, emotional.
        2. Faith is something in and of itself.
        3. Faith is outside control—you have it or you don't.
    B. "All you have to do is believe."
        1. If you believe enough, you can get absolutely anything."
        2. If you don't get what you are after, it's because of a lack of faith.
    C. "Prayer is totally a matter of faith."
        1. This leads to two erroneous conclusions:
            a. If you get what you want, it is because of superior faith.
            b. If you don't get what you want, it is because of lack of faith.
        2. This leads to erroneous practices:
            a. Teaching that you can have anything.
            b. Ignoring the will of God in regard to prayer.
        3. This ignores clear teaching of Scripture—various qualifications for answered prayer beside faith:
            a. Praying in the name of Christ (John 14:13; 16:23).

b. Abiding in Christ (John 15:17).
c. Obedience (1 John 3:22).
d. Accord with His will (1 John 5:14).

III. **The Dimensions of Faith**
  A. Faith is a rational matter.
    1. It is something we decide on.
    2. Lack of faith is condemned ("O ye of little faith") so it must be a matter we can do something about.
  B. Faith is a difficult matter for many of us.
    1. Why are we lacking in faith?
      a. Don't really believe God can do anything.
      b. Afraid God won't want to do what we want done (or the way we want it done).
      c. Don't feel we are deserving of His goodness?
    2. How does our lack show?
      a. We don't pray about things.
      b. We worry and fret.
      c. We live beneath our potential level.
  C. Faith can be grown (Rom. 10:17).
    1. We gain faith from Word of God.
    2. Gain faith through personal experience.
    3. Gain faith from our contact with God's people.

Conclusion:
Faith and prayer obviously go together, but the connection isn't quite as uncomplicated as it seems. There is more to it than faith, but it is impossible without faith!

How to Stay Out of Trouble

Matthew 26:41

Introduction:

It is easy to plunge into difficulty without thought. Jesus urges His people to be cautious.

I. **The Setting**
   A. We don't fully understand all that transpired here.
      1. Surely designed to show us:
         a. Reality of His sufferings.
         b. Intensity of His sufferings.
      2. May have been some aspect of bringing His will fully into accord with the will of the Father.
   B. It was beginning of very trying time for disciples.
      1. He wanted them to stay awake:
         a. For companionship.
         b. Because they were about to face trial.
      2. He wanted to teach them some lessons about the future.

II. **The Statement**
   A. A commandment.
      1. Twofold—watch and pray.
      2. "A summary of the Christian life."
   B. A cause.
      1. "That ye enter not into temptation (testing)."
      2. Has idea of "succumb."
   C. A condition.
      1. "The spirit is willing but the flesh is weak."
      2. Shows necessity of command.

III. **The Stress**
   A. Watch—keep on the alert.
      1. By watching for Satan's attacks and traps.
      2. By avoiding potential problem situations.
      3. By "looking before you leap."
      4. By knowing the Word of God.
      5. By obedience (why experience unnecessary testing and trial brought about by disobedience?).
   B. Pray—keep on praying.
      1. That you will be kept out of temptation and testing.
      2. That you will be kept in temptation and testing.
      3. That you will be safely delivered from temptation and testing.

C. Know your own weakness—the willingness of the spirit and the weakness of the flesh.
   1. The will, mind, spirit is willing, but the flesh is weak.
   2. Had immediate illustration in disciples.
   3. So true of us (Paul knew this truth—Rom. 7:15–21).
   4. Self-confidence is one of our greatest enemies in regard to temptation.

Conclusion:

Some temptation and testing comes our way allowed of God for our spiritual growth and development. Much of the wrong we get into, however, is of our own making. Our problem is that we don't watch (keep on the alert), pray, and give ourselves credit for the evil tendencies we actually have.

The Pattern of Prayer
Luke 11:1–13

Introduction:

The disciples had watched the prayer life of Jesus and saw what they wanted. They said, "Teach us to pray" (not "how" to pray); in response He gave them four pointers.

I. **Pattern** (vv. 2–4)
- A. I have already given you this—remember?
- B. But just a reminder:
  1. "Father"
     - a. Form used by children.
     - b. No one had ever used this before Christ.
  2. Concern for God.
     - a. Conditions rest of prayer.
     - b. Follows Matthew 6:33 (be right with God before asking).
  3. Concern for man.
     - a. Give us—our day by day bread.
     - b. Forgive us—based on our forgiveness—"Forgive us our debts as we *have forgiven* our debtors."
     - c. Lead us—don't seek to escape sin much less temptation.
     - d. Deliver us—we do come upon temptation.
- C. Not necessarily for repetition but no problem with doing so.

II. **Persistence** (vv. 5–8)
- A. Given in parabolic form.
  1. Usually designed to teach or illustrate one truth.
  2. Best not to attempt to fill in too many details.
- B. Lessons of parable.
  1. He went for his friend.
  2. God wants us to exercise great boldness in prayer.
  3. God wants us to continue on in prayer.

III. **Promise** (vv. 9–10)
- A. Form of the promise.
  1. "Keep asking, seeking, finding."
  2. Verse 10 is really a rephrasing for emphasis.
  3. Best to see emphasis in terms rather than in distinctions.

B. The lesson of the promise:
   1. Our prayers cannot be in vain.
   2. God won't give the harmful or the phony to us.
   3. A broad, general promise.
   4. Emphasized because of our lack of faith.

IV. **Provision** (vv. 11–13)
   A. The point of the parable:
      1. Human fathers are good to their children.
      2. If human fathers are like this, how much more God?
   B. The teaching of the parable:
      1. God, more than a human father, gives us good things.
      2. Holy Spirit is best gift of all.

Conclusion:
The child of God ought to see perceptible, daily answers to prayer. Will you make a commitment to getting into prayer until you get an answer?

The Crowbar of Prayer

Luke 11:5–13

Introduction:

Those who are not very skilled mechanically often have certain failure-proof procedures. To make it work: slap it, punch it, bang it, kick it, hammer it, grab a sledgehammer. To get it loose: pry with your fingernails, a screwdriver, a claw hammer, a crowbar. Some people have the same approach to prayer.

I. **An Improper Approach**
    A. Its statement: "Prayer is the crowbar Christians use to pry favors out of a reluctant God."
        1. We have to beg, plead, wheedle, to get answers from God.
        2. It is based on man-centered concept that what we get from God is entirely the result of what we do.
        3. We have to prove that we are serious, earnest, worthy.
    B. Its source—based on two specific passages of Scripture.
        1. Jacob and the angel.
            a. Usual—Jacob trying to break through and overcome God.
            b. Actually reverse: God trying to break through and bless Jacob (no blessing until Jacob broken).
        2. Parable given by Christ in both Matthew and Luke.

II. **A Correct Approach**—"The Savior teaches in a striking manner the certainty of answered prayer, to pray with firm assurance of answers."
    A. Context emphasizes the certainty of prayer being answered.
        1. Begging, pleading doesn't fit the picture in the illustration.
        2. Also doesn't fit the general scope or teaching of the passage.
    B. Translation—KJV "importunity"—begging, pleading, persistence.
        1. Single use in Scripture; can mean something else.
        2. Boldness; come boldly based on friendship.
    C. Interpretation.
        1. Trace the details of the story.
            a. Man has need created by visitor.
            b. Goes to friend seeking help.

        c. Friend—who might not otherwise respond because inconvenient—responds to boldness based on friendship.

        d. If friend will respond—for whatever reason—how much more will the Lord respond to requests of His people.

    2. Stated.

        a. Doesn't teach need to pry things out of God with persistence.

        b. God is more willing to give than we are to get.

        c. Pray not to overcome reluctant God but to lay hold of His willingness.

  D. Support for the interpretation.

    1. Summary found within passage (vv. 9–10).

        a. Ask, seek, knock: continuative in each case.

        b. Not because you have to do it to get things from God, but because God is willing to give.

        c. Keep on going to God because God wants to give you more than you want to get.

    2. Message of the second parable.

        a. Human father won't give anything worthless/harmful to child.

        b. Human father, rather, will give good gifts to children.

        c. If human father will give good gifts, how much more will Heavenly Father give good gifts to His children.

        d. God will even give the Holy Spirit, greatest of all gifts.

    3. Stress of parable and passage: God's tendency/willingness to give; not on our need to "pry it out."

III. Some Applications

  A. God wants to give us more than we want to have.

  B. Entire passage is designed to encourage us to prayer.

  C. We fail to get so much that we could have.

    1. Good things.

    2. Ability to handle not getting what we want.

    3. Ability to endure what we don't want.

Conclusion:

Prayer is not a matter of agonizing before God; it is a matter of earnestly laying hold on God's willingness and desire to give to His children. Don't complicate something marvelously simple.

Don't Faint

Luke 18:1–8

Introduction:

Don't faint, this will be a brief message. Don't faint, we will be out on time. Don't faint, your husband remembered your birthday. "Don't faint" is a common expression. So common, in fact, that Christ used it also.

I. **Confusion**
   A. This parable usually used to illustrate "crowbar" theology—the idea that we have to pry things out of God.
      1. Often tied in with Matthew 7:7–11.
      2. Stress laid on woman's persistence.
   B. Most of this teaching based on misinterpretation of Jacob's wrestling with the angel.
      1. That is usually seen as the struggle to get from God.
      2. That is the actual struggle of God to get from Jacob.
   C. This passage teaches nothing about the necessity of prying things out of God's hands.

II. **Context**
   A. It deals with the last times.
      1. It speaks of return of Christ.
      2. It details some events surrounding that (vv. 22–23, 34–37).
   B. Notice—"but first."
      1. It details the course of this age.
      2. It specifically indicates that times will be difficult.
   C. It follows with parable we should expect it to relate to difficult times or waiting for the Lord's return.

III. **Concept**
   A. "And He spake a parable unto them *to this end*, that men ought always to pray, and not to faint."
      1. It clearly states point of parable.
      2. It fits into context of living in last times.
   B. Details of parable.
      1. Godless judge and wronged widow.
      2. She desired justice ("avenge" me).
      3. She finally wears him down.

C. Notice the intended contrast.
 1. If a totally godless judge can be worn down . . .
 2. How much more will a loving God give justice to His own chosen ones who cry to Him?

IV. Conclusion
A. God will bring justice to His own.
 1. "Who cry day and night unto Him" is statement of fact, not reason why He will avenge.
 2. "Though He bear long with them."
B. He will bring justice speedily.
 1. His timing is always perfect.
 2. Word has atmosphere of "suddenly."
C. God will bring justice to His tried people.
 1. Because they pray, not because of how much they pray.
 2. Final vindication at His appearing but many vindications along the way.
  a. Many things will be dealt with now.
  b. Ultimately, everything will be dealt with.

V. Challenge
A. The facts.
 1. As we wait His coming, things will be difficult (more so as time wears on).
 2. We have two options while waiting: pray or faint (lose heart).
 3. He wants us to pray and encourages us with the assurance that justice will be served.
B. The question.
 1. When the Son of man finally comes, will He find this kind of faith on the earth?
 2. Has to do with a faith that trusts and prays rather than loses heart.
C. The challenge: when times are tough, don't faint—pray as He will surely, ultimately answer.

Conclusion:
We often want to "faint," and many do end up fainting. David understood what is involved here: "I had fainted unless I had believed to see the goodness of the Lord in the land of the living." (Psalm 27:3). Don't faint!

The Man Who Prayed to Himself

Luke 18:9–14

Introduction:

Have you ever known anyone who was always right? Christ ran into that problem during His earthly ministry. Verse 9 in the NIV says: "Now to some self-righteous persons, those who trust in themselves and looked down on everybody else, Jesus told this parable."

I. **Two Men**
   A. A Pharisee
      1. Very religious.
      2. Strict in interpreting the law.
      3. Proud, self-important, "better-than-thou."
      4. Self-righteous.
   B. A Publican
      1. Tax collector.
      2. Tended to be extortioners.
      3. Associated with hated Rome.
      4. Usually low-class rabble.

II. **Two Prayers** (common for Temple to be place of private devotions)
   A. The Pharisee—an incredible prayer.
      1. Bold in brassy sense—stands as close to the Holy Place as he can.
      2. Pre-occupied with self.
         a. Addresses God but never mentions Him again.
         b. Actually "prays with himself"—talks about himself to himself.
      3. Self-vindicating.
         a. Does not deal with major themes: sin, guilt, repentance, forgiveness, etc.
         b. Believes he has no sin to confess.
      4. Filled with comparison/contrast.
         a. "I am not as other men are."
         b. Manages to include Publican in prayer.
         c. Note the kinds of people he compares himself to—not to the best and the brightest.
      5. Focuses on personal achievement.
         a. Works (beyond law's requirements).
         b. Externals (things easily seen).
         c. Peripherals (note essential truths).

B. The Publican—also an incredible prayer.
   1. Humble—stands at a distance.
   2. Contrite—downcast, ashamed of himself and his sin.
   3. Sincere—cries out from depth of being.
   4. Self-accusatory—THE sinner.

III. Two Results
A. One went away full.
   1. Not the one who expected to.
   2. "Justified" has its theological significance here.
B. One went away empty.
   1. Not the one who expected to.
   2. Came full of self and went away same.
   3. Can't be full of self and of God also.

IV. Two Dangers
A. That of becoming like a Pharisee.
   1. A Christian can't be a Pharisee, but can be like one.
   2. Shows up in various ways:
      a. Pre-occupation with self.
      b. Belief that self above sin.
      c. Believe self better than others.
      d. Focus on own works, etc., but no concern with own sins (sins of spirit worse than sins of flesh).
B. That of trusting in one's own righteousness as way to heaven.
   1. Any approach that stresses doing good works or being good enough is exactly what is in view here.
   2. There is nothing in ourselves adequate to get us to heaven—that is only in what Christ has done for us.

Conclusion:
Beware of the influence of the Pharisees. It makes you ugly, ruins your effectiveness, and blinds you to your own sin. Beware of trying to get to heaven on your own righteousness.

Grab Your Bible and Let Us Pray

John 17:17

Introduction:

The Bible undergirds everything else spiritually, and we have much trouble today because of ignoring this truth. We need to put the Bible ahead of every other matter. Grab your Bible, and let us pray!

I.   **The Word of God Informs Prayer**
  A.   It tells us that we should pray.
    1.   Many questions about prayer.
    2.   Basic reason to pray—because Bible says so.
  B.   It tells us what we should pray for.
    1.   Filled with comprehensive listing.
    2.   Philippians 4:6.
  C.   It tells us how we should pray.
    1.   He answered request—teach us to pray.
    2.   We pray to the Father in the name of the Son.

II.   **The Word of God Delineates Prayer**
  A.   It declares the will of God.
    1.   Two levels of revelation: direct/derived.
    2.   The Bible provides the parameters.
  B.   It defines the limits of prayer.
    1.   Prayer outside limits of Word of God pointless.
    2.   Bible defines the will of God.
  C.   It diminishes the scope of prayer.
    1.   Seems strange to speak of diminished prayer.
    2.   Pointless to pray about many things.
      a.   Things assuredly the will of God.
      b.   Things assuredly not the will of God.

III.   **The Word of God Empowers Prayer**
  A.   It encourages us to pray.
    1.   We are given commandments.
    2.   We are given examples.
  B.   It energizes prayer when quoted in prayer.
    1.   Honoring to the Lord to quote Him to Himself.
    2.   Shows that we are conversant with His will.
  C.   It equips us to pray.
    1.   Key criteria for answered prayer—obedience.
    2.   Prayer pointless if not coupled with obedience.

IV. The Word of God Assures Prayer

    A. It contains promises for prayer.
        1. Must be sure of what the promises say.
        2. Must be sure the promises are for us (conditional? rational?).
    B. It contains portraits of answers to prayer.
    C. It contains a philosophy of prayer.
        1. Should pray about everything.
        2. God wants to give us more than we want to get.
        3. The life of the one praying conditions what is secured.
        4. The will of God is the key issue.

Conclusion:

The more our prayer life is based on the Word of God, the more we are likely to achieve in prayer. Possibly we have trouble in prayer because we are not more immersed in the Word. "The Christian who studies the Bible is not searching *for truth* but searching *into* truth."

Prayer and the Will of God

Romans 8:26–27; Psalm 37:4; 1 John 3:22

Introduction:

Most questions concerning the will of God have already been answered by the Word of God. Most of the remaining questions are, "Should I do this or that?" "Should I follow this course or that?" Because we need guidance, the issues of prayer and the will of God frequently collide.

I. **Praying in the Will of God** (Rom. 8:26–27)
   A. We can always say, "Thy will be done."
   B. The Holy Spirit assists us.
      1. We don't know what to pray for as we ought.
         a. What are our real needs?
         b. What are the real needs of others?
         c. What is the will of God respecting these things?
      2. Holy Spirit helps us in prayer.
         a. He searches our hearts and knows our prayers.
         b. He interprets our prayers to God.
         c. He does so according to the will of God.
      3. Does this leave us passive in the matter?
         a. "Help" used here and Luke 10:40 ("Tell her to help me by taking hold of her end of the task").
         b. We are not to be merely passive.
         c. We pray; He takes prayers and makes them effective.

II. **Desiring the Will of God in Prayer** (Psalms 37:4)
   A. "The purpose of prayer is not to get man's will done in heaven, but rather to get God's will done on earth."
   B. Can we expect all the desires of our hearts?
      1. Passage obviously refers to getting requests answered.
         a. "He will grant thee. . . ."
         b. ". . . the things desired, requested?"
      2. "If we delight in the Lord and seek to please Him, then something will happen to our desires."
      3. Our prayers will become a reflection of God's own desires in our hearts (John 4:34).
   C. Finding the will of God in prayer may exact a price.
      1. We need never fear the will of God.
      2. If we are praying in the will of God, we need never fear His answers to us.

III. **Living in the Will of God** (1 John 3:22)
   A. "If we want to pray in the will of God, then we must live in the will of God."
      1. When we live in the will of God, our desires become more and more like His.
      2. "God delights to answer emergency prayers, but living in His will will face us with fewer emergencies."
   B. Living in the will of God tied to:
      1. Accomplishing things in prayer ("unless we are doing the will of God, our living will negate our praying").
      2. Developing a spirit of prayer (1 Thess. 5:17)—"Prayer is not something that we do as much as something that arises out of what we are."
      3. Regular times of prayer—"regular times of prayer make possible a constant attitude of prayer."
   C. Note specific teaching in this passage—verse 23.
      1. The requisite commandments are given here.
         a. Believe
         b. Love one another
      2. Places love on same plane as belief.
      3. Probably more prayer hindered for this reason than for any other.

Conclusion:
If we want to get beyond the superficial in prayer and begin to accomplish serious things, we must take the will of God into account. We must pray in the will of God, desire the will of God above all we pray, and live in accord with the will of God.